RED
ROOM
BAR

A collection of poems by Tomic Riter

This is a work of creative nonfiction.
Some parts have been fictionalized
in varying degrees for various purposes.

First edition

Self-published

Connect with the author
**website – https://tomicriter.in
blog – https://tomicriter.in/blog
instagram @tomic.riter
email – riter.tomic@gmail.com**

God made the world
and then he opened his can of beer
and he sat down
and he said,

'Well, shit!'

. . .

Red Room Bar

**Dedicated
to all the beer drinking
and
to all the beer drinkers
...**

Red Room Bar

Preface

The journey began in 2016, but as it went down in my history, there were stretches of time, really long stretches of time when literally nothing was happening. It was as if I was standing in an infinitely long, waiting for my turn, waiting for my life to begin again, and during all that waiting, a thought, 'What else is there to do?' So I took to drinking. Drinking in cheap bars, drinking while sitting by some lake, drinking all locked up inside my room. It was beer mostly and I preferred to drink alone. This book is a collection of 50 poems, or as I like to call them, 50 bar poems, written over the course of six years i.e. from 2015 to 2020 and written in no particular order. I wrote as I remembered and as I remembered best.

- Tomic Riter

Red Room Bar

Contents

Red Room Bar

X

1. **When I get drunk**

when I get drunk
I accelerate all the way
disregarding my own life,
the significance of it
I let the fuel burn
there are stones in my path
and I will bang into them
and even slip on the road

how bad can it go
when it's already worst

'Take the cigarette with you.
I need only one,' said my boss
earlier this afternoon
I took the cigarette, put in my pocket
cursed my boss and drove home
and later that day, I thought,
I would smoke that one

I have no time to count the clouds
alcohol has fused my both eyes
and now, my jaws are getting bloody
and they ache
they ache like my teeth will start falling
any time now

not long before I am on a stretcher
waiting for a final cut in my body

waiting for nobody
to pay for my medical expenses.

Red Room Bar

2. **Drinking alone**

on the other side of the curtain
cricket match is playing on TV
drunkards shouting, cheering, cursing

'Are you waiting for somebody?'
asked the boy waiter after looking
at the rum bottle,
all sealed and looking like
it's waiting for somebody
to open it

I nod in NO
I utter no word
I am not waiting for anybody
I am capable of drinking alone

I got that rum bottle from a military man
who he is, I got no idea
never seen him
only later, I got to know that it was his father
who was in military and who is now dead
and so each month, he gets two bottles
of whiskey
for free
the man himself doesn't drink
so sometimes, he sells free whiskey
to men like me

the boy waiter said nothing else,
went away and closed

Red Room Bar

the cabin curtain behind him

he didn't return until late,
until I asked him
to bring me the goddamn bill.

Red Room Bar

3. **To midnight**

swinging drunk
in my chair

few moments to midnight

and then another day

how long before this life is over

but I equally fear another life,
the one coming after this one

a man would only want to live so long

meanwhile, the song changes

whatever the new song is,
I find something in it,
something to live by

meanwhile, the people fall asleep
the wind cools down,
the dust tries to settle down

the stars switch off one by one

I wait for the last light to vanish
after which I guess I will slither back
into my red room.

4. **Few hours ago, in a bar**

I was about to write something
when suddenly, it all vanished

few hours ago,

in a bar

I was waiting for a few more bastards,
they never come on time,
even for drinking beer

you came and then disappeared
and then you came again
and disappeared again
and while I finished alone the upper half
of my first bottle,
you disappeared one more time

the bastards arrived -
all three of them
and we ordered some beer

and soon after,
a salesman arrived

WHAT THE HELL!
WHAT FUCKING MADNESS!
A SALESMAN AT 7 IN THE EVENING
ON A FUCKING SATURDAY
SELLING BEER!

Red Room Bar

'I know you are drinking a good beer, sir,
a really good beer I must tell you,
but believe me, sir, this beer will throw
you off your chair,
it's that fucking good HA HA HA HA'
he said pointing to the bottle in his hand

it was some newly launched beer
that he was trying to sell to us bastards

he himself was drunk on some really bad spirit

'I know you want the premium brand,
I know you want the best,
I know that by looking at your face,'
he told me enthusiastically while looking
at my face

I was wearing a headgear
and I was wearing no spectacles
often, I remove my spectacles while drinking
he must be thinking I was some rich brat

he shook our hands multiple times
while he sold his bullshit to us

before walking away, he offered us
a beer bottle
for free

we drank everything without caring about
what it was

Red Room Bar

and then we ate like wild animals
and finally, we headed to our homes,

me alone and completely
out of my head.

Red Room Bar

5. **A shitty brew pub in a shitty city**

fucking losers
fighting over what to eat
what to watch
where to go to
what to drink
what to talk about

nobody cared except me
about whether or not
there was a bar nearby

'You are leaving so early, sir?
You came only just now…'

'Your customer service is shit.
The drink doesn't matter that much to me.
I can drink anywhere. But I walked
five fucking kilometers to here
because I heard you brew your own beer,
which is totally shit,' I told the bartender

and then I walked back
five kilometers
and ate a simple meal
and then I walked back to my hotel room
without any desire
to drink that night.

Red Room Bar

6. **Four men in a bar**

one is sipping and then smiling,
smiling on I do not know what
nothing exists in front of him

the second one is staring at a glass of rum –
his glass of rum
he is stirring it slowly,
and as the stirring continues,
he is getting lost more and more
into something,
what is that something, I do not know

the third one is having nothing
he is just sitting with folded hands
he is not a drunkard

the fourth one
is draining his second glass of beer
and reading chronicles of Bob Dylan
and listening to some slow jazz

I am the fourth one

outside, it's afternoon
and Dylan writes,

'Outside the wind was blowing,
straggling cloud wisps, snow whirling
in the red lanterned streets,
city types scuffling around, bundled up –

Red Room Bar

salesmen in rabbit fur earmuffs
hawking gimmicks, chestnut vendors,
steam rising out of manholes.
None of it seemed important.'

I put down the book
and drink a little more and look around

nothing like what he describes exists here
NOTHING!

meanwhile, the fifth one
enters the bar
GODDAMNIT!
and he sits right in front of me

'Got a lighter?' he asks me
'I don't smoke. The waiter there has got
matchsticks,'
I tell him

'What's that book? Oh Dylan.
You are reading here in a bar like this?
This is a shit place,' he blabbers
and lights a cigarette.

I pick up my book again

I am the only one here writing,
just like it was when I came here
last time.

that was on Christmas

Red Room Bar

the year was 2020

the bar closed at nine
that night.

Red Room Bar

7. **Excesses**

I am getting heavier

and heavier

and heavier

what have they mixed in my drink???

FUCKING PIGLETS!

sitting in this shimmering hell

on a Thursday evening

my home is miles away

and tomorrow, it will be light years away

and I won't lie – right now,

I can't see shit!

Red Room Bar

8. **Beer on repeat**

I repeat beer after
beer after beer

I repeat

there are moments in life
which you want they go on
forever

for me, it's nothing much
but drinking beer
all by myself in some corner
of a bar glowing not too bright

sometimes, I got to turn off
the bulb myself
I need to get up from my chair,
walk to the bulb, twist it,
remove it from its holder and toss it
out of the window

it sets the mood for the rest
of the night

me waiting for nobody
nobody waiting for me

mother will call in some time
to check if I am still alive

Red Room Bar

she does that everyday

I will tell her lies, just like every day,

that everything here is going fine.

Red Room Bar

9. **No fun drinking in a glass**

the bar boy asks if I need
a glass
to pour my beer

I nod in no

I drink straight from the bottle
or can or whatever that holds
that pungent elixir

'No fun drinking in a glass,'
the boy says and laughs

I nod in yes and laugh
and as he keeps mumbling,
I grab the bottle by its neck
and wrap my lips around its mouth
and take a long wide deep swig

ending another shit day.

Red Room Bar

10. **Insanity**

any man having a sane mind
would not go from gym
straight to a bar

but if any man does so,
I understand him

I have been there
a thousand times

and I am still there.

Red Room Bar

11. **Kerouac**

one beer can down

I suddenly remember Kerouac's words

Climb that goddamn mountain
Climb that goddamn mountain

Climb that goddamn fucking mountain!

Red Room Bar

12. **Un-bar**

everything is flowing,
to where, I got no idea

'Sir, you have come here
after a long time!' said the boy barber

'I know. I don't like grooming.
Just trim the beard and leave
the rest as it is,' I replied
to the boy who is always
too enthusiastic
to know what's going on

'Sure, sir. Sure,' he replied
and I sat in the chair

and it didn't take long

and I didn't like to be there for long

it wasn't a bar
it wasn't a bookshop

it was just a barber shop
the owner's face was half swollen
his one eye was popping out dangerously
he looked like two men in one
I wanted to ask him what happened
to his face but I didn't
I paid him and left from there

Red Room Bar

on the way back home,
I stopped at a roadside spot
completely dark
and I thought about where to go next

nothing really came in my head.

Red Room Bar

13. **Drank and drove**

you are watching my skin
how brightly your eyes are shining

I had no idea at what speed I was riding

must be 80 kmph at least
I stamped a rabbit,
cut a dog in two
not a scream from their mouths
not a battle from their end
their souls flew off to heaven quietly
and at once

life stops in its own way
but salvation can sometimes be found
only at the bottle of a beer bottle
and in all the talks you do
while you are drunk
and you can still hear and talk

'Sir, what will you eat?' the boys asked me
'Don't worry about me,' I told them
and let them go and have a fine dinner

my path was another I had to ride alone
and it really didn't matter
how many of them
knew me or understood me.

Red Room Bar

14. **Back in time**

how long before I go out and grab another beer?
An hour? Four hours? A night? Two days?
two days seems to be the answer

but there's no answer to 'why'
why two days? why not six?

actually, two days feels just right
I need a little dizziness now and then

now, it would be foolish to say
that the dizziness helps in writing
even beer doesn't help
it really doesn't help with anything
it only tells you that things could have been
much worse
but they are not

so why not grab a beer now and drink it.

Red Room Bar

15. **I continue drinking**

I continue drinking
until late night
to forget the significance of this day,
to forget all that happened on this day

'Are you back home?' mother called
a few hours ago and asked the same thing
for the eleventh time
this week.

'No, mother. I am crawling in a gutter
and it's pretty here.
Why do you ask?'

people live unconsciously
their thoughts, sentences keep repeating
without their knowledge,
without any control

only the calendar date keeps changing
otherwise, it's all the same
right to the very fucking end.

Red Room Bar

16. **The problem**

half the problem lies in being drunk.

the other half lies in not being drunk.

Red Room Bar

17. **Red all the time**

red light room
inside which
I am my own god and destroyer

jumping on tracks, forgetting to make
my own heart beat

a swig of fresh cold beer can do
something about these things
it can make you forget about how
you waited for hours
before the gates to heaven opened,
before you were allowed in,
before the good times when all was hell
and anything seemed to hurt
and it hurt like it was final
and you felt like there was no life
beyond that kind of hurt

I grab a book and put it on my face
as I lay naked in the red light
and I refuse to read s single word

today was the day I wouldn't want again

I am writing about it first and last
before I crash into some dream.

Red Room Bar

18. **To the same old bar**

5:15 evening, roaming around
in gym like a stray dog
when I recognize the owner
of the bar where I usually go

he was panting
he was unable to walk
and his stomach was flat on the ground

'Hey!' he waved at me as soon as he saw me

'When did you join?' I asked him smiling

'It's been two or three days. It's hard here.
Drinking is a lot easier. HA HA…'

indeed, it is

6:15 evening, driving through
the market streets
people buying stuff, selling stuff

I bought nothing and sold nothing
and I drove right on their footprints
as the red sun readied to drown
behind a gigantic hospital building

I kept driving and finally stopped at the bar
whose owner I had met at the gym

Red Room Bar

I entered the bar

the waiter saw me and recognized me
'Which cabin?' I asked him with hand gestures
he understood and said 'Number 26.'
I looked at the cabin number 26
Cabin number 28 would have
made me happier
but number 26 was good enough too

I entered the cabin, sat on the bench
the bench opposite to mine was vacant
I went there alone

'One Budweiser pint, please,' I told the waiter
as soon as he entered my cabin

at 6:50 evening, I ordered another pint
and I was listening to some really slow music
that was playing on the television
that they had
and I thought,

'This is good. This part of this shit life.
Me being here and having a drink quietly
and listening to some sweet slow music
that offers a kind of high
you just cannot ignore.'

the thought stopped there
and I began drinking my second pint
and I began to think about what to eat that night

Red Room Bar

that town hadn't any great chefs
or great restaurants
but a couple of places did exist that offered
lethally good food

but for some reason, I didn't want
to go anywhere else that night
I called the waiter
the boy entered my cabin

I ordered boiled chicken salted
I avoid eating exotic unless
someone else is paying

on most days,
a skinned chicken boiled
does the job pretty well

7:40 night, paying the bill,
pissing on brown grass
and then driving back home

Robert Johnson was playing some
lonesome real blues for me

what more did I need –
a smooth enough road to drive on
and some fine music
to make it easy on the bumps and potholes

I reached my bungalow,
opened the main gate –

Red Room Bar

a giant slider iron gate that had rusted badly
around the corners

wasps had gathered in mad dancing
around the white lamp that I had left
burning on the porch

I entered, locked the door,
lifted a chair from the drawing room
and walked upstairs to the roof

I sat in the chair in the middle of roof
and placed my legs on the boundary wall

and I looked up and exhaled deeply

the moon was constructing itself back
to a full glow

I thought about the rum bottle downstairs
and that that place, the place where I was living,
wasn't as bad as the people
had told me it would turn out to be

in short – trust nobody's words and thoughts
and opinions

experience everything yourself.

Red Room Bar

19. **Happy birthday!**

sometimes, I do noble things after getting drunk

'Here, sir. Have a piece of cake!'
he said holding in his hands a platter
full of white cake with a lot of cream on top
all sliced up and ready to be thrown
to some of us drunk dogs

'Why? What's the occasion?' I enquired
'It's Kyle's birthday today! He works with us.'

'Tell him I greeted him!' I replied
and took a piece of cake and ate at once
it was delicious!

what's not delicious when you get drunk
you can eat horseshit and call it
the best meal of your life

it was at this point of time
when I began writing this one

few minutes later, Kyle entered
my cabin
the birthday boy!
he entered along with the man
who brought me cake

'Sir, this is Kyle,' said the guy
who brought me cake

Red Room Bar

'Oh I know you. I just forget names,'
I said laughingly, they both laughed as well
'Happy birthday!' I greeted Kyle
and shook his hands

about my own birthday, I do not give a damn
but that night, when I was drunk
and I wished that man and he smiled,
I found something extremely real
in that smile

I can even conclude that in that moment,
that man felt really happy
and for a moment, although I was drunk
then and I am drunk even now as I write this,
I felt happy as well

'Would you like a beer now?' I asked Kyle.
'Oh no no no. I am on duty, sir.
Besides, I do not drink,' he replied
with a smile

'Fair enough. Have a good time,' I said
and shook his hands again
and he went away.

I have met a lot of waiters waiting
in bars who have never been drunk

I have also met men who will put
their filthy mouths right on a sewage outlet
to experience a moment's high

Red Room Bar

there exist both kinds
and all kinds in between them

that night, drunk in thatbar,
I thought about all those kinds
and I wondered whether to order
another bottle or not

I guess I already had enough.

Red Room Bar

20. **For a pint of beer**

back in my beloved bar
for a pint of beer
after downing a fat burger
and a bowl of fries already

on television, some silly song
from 1980s is playing too loud
three drunks are listening to it
I am not one of them
I have my earphones on but the television song
is so loud and silly, I can hear it clearly

I won't be here for long or so I think
I have got a great book waiting back
at my home to read
and more jazz to listen to

I have got to clean all the dirt
before it's too late
I have got to head out
and drink some fresh early day air

'Anything else?' the waiter is enquiring
'Nothing more today,' I am telling him
he is a far better listener than all the
friends and family I ever had

all the waiters waiting
in all the bars
are far better listeners

Red Room Bar

I can guarantee you that much.

21. **One silent evening**

a quick run to the bar

I won't be sitting there today

I would buy the beer bottles
and bring them home

my fridge is working fine now
the ice is forming
the water in the water bottles
is getting colder

all fine

I bought four beer bottles
and stacked them inside the fridge
right away

some warm rice and egg curry
and a glass of fresh beer made
for a fine dinner.

Red Room Bar

22. **Nothing better could be done**

after eight long months,
sold all my 85 beer bottles
to a scrap dealer whom I made
a phone call
at 4 in the evening

he paid me 100 bucks for all 85 bottles

'What to do with those 100 bucks,' I thought
so I went to the same old bar
at 7 evening
and bought myself a beer bottle
and around 8 night I started to leave
when the bar manager, who knew me better
than my own parents did, came to me
and smiled and asked

'Leaving so early today! I thought you
would stay until late.
It's Saturday…'

'Saturday??? Where the hell
did my Friday go???' I thought
without saying anything,
no surprise on my face,
only a big laugh blasted right away

I paid the bill and drove home
inebriated, elated

Red Room Bar

I got down my bike, parked it,
and as I began ascending
those six flights of stairs
to my room,
I saw two fat women staring at
the transformer that short-circuited
last night

and I wished,

I wished that they touched
the transformer
and be fried to lumps of shit.

23. **And I wrote all of this**

a quite day after years, I guess

it's like I have stepped out
of a cruel hurricane
I hear nothing except
the sweet silence
singing
only if all my days were this quiet,
but that's not happening

at 6:45 evening, I am on the road again,
driving,
and a giant wasp hits my forehead
and created a hole

'I am leaving on February 1st,'
I called my landlord
at exact 5:12 evening and told him that

'Fine. You were always a problem, Mr. Riter.
Always a problem.
I hope you aren't returning after that,'
my landlord replied
at exact 5:13 that same evening

'No. I won't be returning.
I have found a better place,'
I told him and cut the call

I had found my paradise and there,

Red Room Bar

I would be playing alone
and I would be happier,
or so I thought

at 7:35 evening, back in bar
for a pint of beer
two men sitting across me
recognize me and laugh
I recognized one of them
but I pretended I didn't
and I didn't laugh at all

I drank my beer and talked to nobody
and munched on two chocolate bars
that I had bought an hour ago
and I listened to nothing else
except the sweet jazz that was
fucking my eardrums

and I wrote all of this.

Red Room Bar

24. **On drinking**

people here care to eat something good
only on festivals

11 in the morning but not a man in sight
where has everybody gone?
I heard they are worshipping some god
for some kind of well-being

it's the same world today
as it was back in those days
when you were born
nothing changes except you –
growing older and one day, disappearing

that's the only pleasure you can have –
the pleasure of disappearing

7:55 evening,
sitting alone in the same old bar,
corner seat, gulping down some beer,
thinking about a trip
from where I won't ever return
'Soon,' I am thinking,
'Maybe on the coming weekend…'

12:15 noon,
I was offered a fair deal, which
I accepted seven minutes later

I hate the thinking part of things

I do things and then I forget
I forget all the time

remembering is a tiring business

the third time you meet anybody,
you already know what and how about them

it's a fucking disaster to know anything
about anybody

in oblivion is real pleasure,
but by the time you realize that,
you also realize that
you have already wasted more than a half
of your life
and masturbated on all of your nights
and half of your days.

Red Room Bar

25. **Miles away**

waking up at 3:45 morning
what the hell!

at 6 morning, travelling to Pine City
in a cab with three more travellers,
I know one of them,
the other two are looking outside for
most of the time

at 7:15 morning,
standing at the edge of a cliff,
taking a piss that disturbs the fog
lying on the ground

at 10, arrived and standing
in front of a bus that refuses to move

at 12 noon, dead from hunger and thirst
and poor sleep yesterday night
'But all that can wait until evening,'
I tell myself

at 2 o'clock noon, in another bus
to another city
for the same work that could have finished
in the first city

at 3:15 noon, possibility of rain
but nothing falls from above
at 4:30 evening, arrived

Red Room Bar

at 6, in my hotel room
at 7, in the hotel bar
and it's already crowded
and there's no music, no television,
and each one of them is shouting so loudly
for God know what!

'One Budweiser strong, please,
and a bowl of peanuts,' I tell the waiter
and say nothing else and wait

8 at night, the bar is fairly lit
the shouts have silenced for a while

'You are a nice man. I know you are.
You are our guest here.
Don't worry about anything.
You can sit in the section reserved for families
if the noise inside the bar bothers you.
Only you can't drink there…'
the hotel owner told me a while ago

'Oh it's fine. The noise won't bother me,'
I replied him
and headed downstairs to the bar

I am no nice man
I am just too tired to talk rudely,
too tired to talk anything
and the only good that I did
was paying the hotel room bill upfront

I am miles away from my home

Red Room Bar

and there's no going back
until next morning,
so I might as well behave a little
for a night
and get my ass saved
in this strange strange city.

26. **Really, I do not remember**

always much cooler to occupy a corner seat
in a bar and watch as things unfold

'You looked tensed, sir. You should relax,'
a good friend told me earlier
that evening.

'I am trying,' I told him
and I could tell him only so much

that evening, we talked for a couple of hours
and drank four pints of beer

9:11 night and I do not know where I am
or what I am doing here
I am here probably for food
because all I see around is men eating
lots of men and lots of eating going on
like from tomorrow,
it's starvation days for everybody
HA HA HA HA

I occupy a seat, order bread and butter to eat
there's a man sitting on the floor,
eating shit, and he looks up at me
and shakes his head,
as if asking me,
'What you looking at, motherfucker?'

I quickly turn my head away from him

Red Room Bar

and wait for my order

and as I wait, I think again

'When did I step out of the bar?'

Red Room Bar

27. **Abuse**

over the years,
all that pain and hurt
has drowned in beer and rum
and all that has remained
is dizziness
and more dizziness
and this fiery desire to drink
and drink
and keep drinking
as my day approached my night.

Red Room Bar

28. **As usual**

work at 10 o'clock morning,
as usual

I always reach early
I reach at 9 o'clock morning
and I remember having lunch
at 1 o'clock noon

and whatever happens in between,
I am sure it happens everyday

work until 5:15 evening at which time,
I remember I need to leave for home

the sky is clouded all day
it only adds to the dullness of everything
it is even raining
I am even getting wet

7 in the evening and it's raining ferociously
and I am on my bike driving to the same old bar,
and before that, to the same old gym,
the only gym in this town, in fact

it's almost 8 at night and I am going
straightaway
to that hell of a bar -
my only lifeline here –
for a pint of peer and a bowl of salted peanuts
and a quiet corner where nothing bad happens.

Red Room Bar

29. **Who needs a television!**

sitting alone in the red room bar,
munching on some roasted shit

'Kid, you got to wear your mask properly
or I will fuck you up,' says a drunk man
to the boy waiting on these tables

a man walks in , buys a can of Tuborg Strong,
opens it in a hurry, spills half on the table
I take a note of it as I drink my beer in no hurry
he finishes the other half quickly and walks out
disappointed and to some extent, embarrassed

some movie is running on the television
that is mounted on the wall right
in front of my eyes

'Why don't you turn it off?'
I say to the boy waiter

'What? What are you saying?' the boy replies

'Nevermind,' I say

I am in no mood to say the same thing twice

I am dreaming of going back to my room
and reading something great
and before that,
a little drinking will be all.

Red Room Bar

30. **Not in this way**

tear me apart with a spear
curse me until I bleed out of my both ears
I am built in a way
I am forged with lovelessness
I am shot in the head and for what,
I really cannot say
your spite for me is supreme poison
and if that doesn't kill me,
then I have to drinking anyways
I am drinking and laughing
and all the drunks have gathered around me,
bowing down and chanting hymns
and the waiter is asking me to leave
and soon all the waiters will be gathering
around me and lifting me up
and throwing me out of here
because soon, it's eleven at night
and after eleven at night , you cannot exist here,

at least not in such a miserable way.

Red Room Bar

31. **Merry Christmas!**

another bar for loners
I like it here

'One Budweiser mild, please.'

'What else, sir?' asks the waiter

'Oh I do not know. Whatever's good to eat,
order a plate of it,' I replied

the best reply of that evening
it's Christmas and all the Santas
are in the toilets,
vomiting out their guts

it's fucking Christmas
so let's fucking celebrate
a tall beer glass
and a poison pill in the shape of a candy
and of course, a bowl of peanuts
yeah, that much will do

I like it here
no crowd, only five or six men
each sitting on separate tables
buried in their cellphones

I guess I am the only one
writing.

Red Room Bar

32. **One after another**

drank another half bottle
Cohen was singing
I let the devil make its way out of me
I fell down a flight of stairs singing the last line
and when I got up, I had blood on my lips
and on a couple of those stairs

I got up and dangled my way
out of that shithole I called my home

I got up and I was sad for something
and I laughed and cleared my eyes of tears

after a long long long fucking time,
a lot had happened in a single day.

Red Room Bar

33. **Without you**

your silence is biting me everywhere

it makes me want to drink
until I throw up

and finally, fall asleep.

Red Room Bar

34. **Drunk on a bad day**

there are bad days,

and then, there was today.

Red Room Bar

35. **Just tired**

'You drunk?'

'Yeah. Just a little,' I said

I was so drunk I couldn't identify anything

I was lost somewhere inside my head

'What happened?'

I looked in nobody's eyes
and I smiled and I said

'Nothing really. I am tired. That's all.'

36. **The red room bar**

red follows blue
follows green
follows red again

a single white lamp hangs down
from the ceiling
like an electric testicle
35, 36, 34 – each wall is numbered
I don't know why
and I didn't realize this yesterday
or the day before that

a fan is mounted on the wall numbered 35
it blows wind where nobody ever sits

forget about drinking there
forget about drinking anywhere else
because all the drinking is right here
in this red room bar

where stacks of boxes filled
with empty beer bottles
lay everywhere
and the bar manager shouts at a bar waiter
and orders him to fill the refrigerator
with more fresh beer bottles

where men arrive with angry heads
and leave with red eyes and sour tongues
and bellies full of beer and wild animals

Red Room Bar

where at every corner sits a waiter
until his name is called and
something is ordered,
but until then, there's no point
in his being alive

we are all saints here
especially after the first beer bottle finishes
and the first stick of smoke burns out

we are all saints here
waiting for our turns to speak out
all the truth
in one single breath or two

squeezed in this hour of this day
on this table right here
is all the drinking happening

and right now, I really cannot think
about any other place
as glorious and as damned
as this one.

Red Room Bar

37. **End**

me and jazz alone
the sky blazed twice as I smoked,

drunk, leaning against a door
that opened to the balcony
and it was inviting in
rain, wind , all of that
which was blowing outside,
falling outside

I tapped my cigarette lightly
the ashes fell on the wet floor below
and made a black pool out of fresh rainwater

Charlie Parker was playing *Summertime*
but it wasn't summer
and Charlie Parker was long dead and gone
and it was raining then just like it was raining
the other day

- a miserable end to a nothing of a day.

Red Room Bar

38. **For nothing**

that day, I and Skril rode 30 miles
for nothing
because when we reached there,
there was nothing there
except closed children parks
and closed wine shops and closed restaurants
and closed motorcycle showrooms
and everything closed

Skril is a good friend of mine and he drinks
sometimes
and he never smokes

on the way back, we stopped at a permit room
it didn't matter whether or not
that place was open
we had to stop somewhere for beer
we had to stop somewhere to forget the fact that
the place where we had gone to turned out
to be nothing and a complete waste of time

so we thought,

'Better to stop somewhere
and at least have a cold beer.'

but the permit room building was all locked up,
its main entrance in chains
no light coming out of its glass windows

Red Room Bar

the 1 o'clock noon sun was making
everything much worse
and it was heating badly
the back of our necks

towards the side of the building,
saw a window left open
we walked to the window
and saw a man sitting inside the building
with all the lights and fans switched off
he was selling alcohol without permission

it didn't matter

I went to the window and bought two cans
of Tuborg Strong and we rode off quickly
to a nearby lake that still had
some rainwater left

we sat on the rocks lying around the pond,
opened our beer cans and began
gulping down the golden fluid
and we sat there in absolute silence
and even the sun had somehow softened
and soon we were drunk again and joyful
and in those joyful moments,
none of that disgust from the hours wasted
in mindless travelling
seemed to matter

I finished my can, tore it into two
and then we rode off to our homes
and I slept for the rest of my life.

Red Room Bar

39. **Just Cohen singing and me drinking**

a poet recites the matters of a heart
one day's suffering isn't enough
but a silent simmering,
sometimes decade-long

rain reminds me of rotten things,
of things rotting
any rain falling on any day rots anything

a great poet dies quietly, unable to go mad
and hence, unable to live and hence,
unable to die properly

unable to proceed further in this evening,
I pour myself a half glass of beer
nothing will grow out of these walls
nothing will astonish me
I remember few lies from years past
and feel the headache rising

I listen to him again and again
and it opens, again, the abyss in me
and, again, I fall gladly into it
and I do not know why but nothing
more true has been written down
and sung loud
about the matters of a heart.

Red Room Bar

40. **I understand it**

the bar boy keeps asking me
'Anything else you need, sir?'

'No. That will be it,' I keep replying him
and then I gulp thrice
and then I call the bar boy
again
and order some more silly snacks
again

he comes back to my table
in another few minutes

'Anything you need, sir?'

he keeps popping up at my table
that's his job
and I understand it
I understand it
better than half the shit of this world

he keeps asking me if I need anything else
and by asking that, he keeps me
from falling asleep

he is barely twelve and he is trying
and I am trying as well
and I keep ordering more snacks
without paying attention
to how much I have ordered

and if I can eat more

'Anything you need, sir?'

'No. I am fine. I will call you
if I need something.'

I finish my glassful and then I pour again
and the cycle continues for several hours

it's just another cheap bar
at the foot of lonely rocky mountain
where only a few come and those who come,
they keep coming back
but no one keeps coming back
as often as me

I hold my head in my hands
and finish another glass
and I send away the boy once again

he runs off to other tables,
undrunk and young and undestroyed,
fighting all the heartlessness
in this corner of the world.

Red Room Bar

41. **Gone to hell**

8 at night
raining outside
I am inside,
a beer bottle in my hand
and it's quarter empty

light goes off as I light a smoke
there's a song in my ears,
its singer unknown, forgotten

I am a saint who needs
his daily dose of something

it's too hot now
too hot, unbearably hot
I remove all my clothes
and take another big gulp
and wait for a little light
but nothing is glowing,
not even those god-made stars hanging
somewhere up there

outside my room is a whole bunch of people
their arrival is my demise

starting tomorrow, things will be different
more crates of beer to get through
days and nights and evenings

twenty minutes pass

Red Room Bar

impossible but it has happened
and it has happened just now

a minute later,
the lights are back!

I begin to lose sight

some old man is emptying his ash tray
in my mouth
while he sings to me
a wonderful sweet lonely song

I turn off all the lights
half a bottle more to go
and after that,

I am gone straight to hell.

Red Room Bar

42. **First ride**

my first ride on Enfield

Skril was driving for the most time
I was just on the pillion seat,
looking around

our destination was a town Kofur
220 kilometres from our place of living
so we started really early in the morning,
I guess we started at 5 in the morning
and it was so cold
and all our fellow countrymen
were still asleep

I started my Enfield at 4:30 morning,
rode from my home to Skril's
it was a short 4 kilometres ride,
half of the route with no roads

I reached his home
we packed a small bag
and hopped back on my Enfield
and started our 4 hour long journey

on the way,
nothing much except small mountains
and mud trails connecting roads

the chilly mist didn't lift
until 8 in the morning

Red Room Bar

by that time, we were halfway through

we reached Kofur around 9:30 morning

by 1 o'clock noon,
we were pretty tired and thirsty
and we began searching for a bar

'I saw one on our way up the mountain,'
I said to Skril
so we began our descent down the mountain

after riding for 15 minutes or so,
we found a little signboard in red
and on it, written in bold white were the words
'BEER AVAILABLE'

we stopped there
we didn't know if that was even a bar
because really, nothing was in plain sight
no man, no bottles, nothing

Skril went inside the little shop
a woman was sitting there

'Got beer?' Skril asked

'Yes. At the back,' replied the woman

'Back where?' Skril enquired

'There…' she said pointing at a mud house
with a tin shed for a roof

Red Room Bar

it was next to that little shop

'Really? That one?' Skril enquired again

'Yes. Just park your motorcycle
behind the house.'

'Sure,' Skril replied

I was already on my way to that mud house
Skril parked the motorcycle as close as possible
to the house
and then, we entered the house

inside was a single fridge stacked
with all kinds of beer
we were thrilled and amused to watch that

'Is this even legal? You selling beer like this?'
I asked the man at the counter
the counter was nothing much
but a single wood desk
and a broken chair behind it
on which sat the man

'Not really.' he replied

'What if the cops come?' I asked

'They won't. Now, what will you have?'
he asked

we took two cans of Pilsner

Red Room Bar

and some snacks and paid

it wasn't a large room
and there was dust all around
whirling
not a chair or a table
it was just the room, totally empty

two men were already sitting in one corner
on the mud floor
they were having whiskey

we sat in another corner, opened our cans,
took large swigs
it was refreshing and at the same time, crazy
nobody would believe in such a place
as that one
it was a little heaven in the middle
of a goddamn nowhere

we sat and drank our beers in peace

'Where have you come from?' asked one
of the two men
who were drinking whiskey

Skril replied

'Just travelling?' he asked again

'Yeah. Pretty much. It's weekend...'
Skril replied

Red Room Bar

I said nothing
I was tired and the beer was quite powerful
we finished our cans and then bought
two cans of Budweiser and some more snacks

'You have come here quite early.
It's fucking noon.
You should stay here for the night.
This place is beautiful at night
and pleasantly cold. During the day,
it's just too fucking hot.
After five in the evening,
it's heavenly,' the man told us
and sipped his whiskey

'Really? We had no idea,' Skril replied

I was completely lost,
watching the dust flow,
listening to everything,
not saying a word

they continued talking for half an hour
and then the two men left
and entered a band of boys,
all four of them
and they sat next to us
and ordered beer

'It's great. Fucking great.
Drinking here like this. Fucking great!'
I told Skril and we both laughed very loud

Red Room Bar

and soon the boys got drunk
and started talking
and that lasted for another hour

after which, we shook hands
with each of those boys

'Have a good time,' I told them
and then we left from there

within an hour of leaving that heaven
we were all flushed out and sleepy
and we drove back like zombies

and it was quite late at night when I unlocked
the door of my home, removed all my clothes

and finally crawled into my bed.

43. **Something wasn't right**

'Which cabin?' I asked the boy waiter
who by then knew me quite well

'Sorry sir. All cabins are occupied?'

'Really? All cabins?'

'You can check for yourself.'

'Fine. Fine. And cabins at the back?'

'They are vacant and available.'

I walked to the cabins at the back
the bar owner was playing with his feral dog
all the back cabins were empty,
lifeless,
quiet like they never grew a tongue

I occupied the second cabin
it had two benches, a little fan
its wires all naked and running down to the
circuit board

'Does the fan work?' I asked the waiter
as soon as he came to take the order

he said nothing and switched on the fan
and it whirled like a toddler

Red Room Bar

'Bring me a bottle of the cheapest beer,'
I told the waiter
he went away

I finished beer in no time

something was not right
sitting there, drinking
it was just too silent

the cabins at the front, where I usually drank
were more happening
and I knew the waiters waiting in that section

this was a strange place,
like a different bar altogether
and the waiters were dead and old and defective

I finished my beer and went to the main counter
'How much?'

'You leaving so early,' said the bar manager

'It's the cabins. They aren't the same.
I like drinking in the cabins at the front,'
I told the bar manager

I paid and didn't talk much after that

it was not really about the drinks

it was about the whole thing
the life happening around

Red Room Bar

and why to stay there

where nothing much
was really happening.

Red Room Bar

44. **What the hell**

I was on a job training
in some XYZ city

it was a 7 days long schedule
with 9 hours of classes each day
from 9 morning to 6 evening

on my first day itself,
I began searching for a bar near to my hostel

nothing for two days
on the third day, I found a little establishment
that was adjacent to a wine shop

only it was a big hall with just a lamp glowing
and you could walk inside with
your beer or whatever
and stand there and drink
no chairs, no tables, no cabinets or anything
the floor was all too dirty and there was garbage
lying all around –
empty bottles, cigarette packs, needles,
plastic bags,
broken lighters, sperm

from my third day onwards, I started going there
I bought beer, walked inside
that little sacred space,
watched the evening raining
and drank my beer

Red Room Bar

'Is there a bar nearby?' a friend asked me on the
next day
and I told him about the sacred space

and the very next day, he brought with him
15 more people
and the place wasn't sacred anymore
because I couldn't drink in peace anymore
and somebody was chattering all the time
and talking bullshit
and the rain added to the hurt because I couldn't
walk home
and I had to be there with all 15 of them
until the rain stopped,
I felt stuck

the next day, a friend gave me weed
and we rolled and smoked in a narrow alley
where the cops wouldn't come
and then we walked to the sacred space
and bought ourselves beer and started drinking
when 25 more people walked in with my friend
whom I had told
about the sacred space

now, he was ruining it not just for me
but for everyone
I walked to him and told him
'What the hell is going on?'

'These are my friends!' he replied

'I don't give a shit!' I said
 and finished my beer in a corner
and I went out of there
and that was the last time I went there

I still remember that place
I hope they have fixed it a little
the rainwater came rushing in straight away

and half the fun is gone when you are drinking
while standing

and your feet are all getting wet.

Red Room Bar

45. **And so it began**

that evening, I was maybe 17 years old
and my head was always buzzing,
not with migraine or anything but by just
looking
at what the other lads and ladies were doing
with their lives –
nothing was making sense

I and Kail, then a friend, balder
and older than me,
were on some street doing something,
I cannot remember clearly what
all I remember now is a small beer shop
holed inside an off-white brick wall
on the left side of the street

we were waiting for the sky to grow darker
there was no place anywhere to sit
or even stand properly on two feet
we were wearing whatever clothes we had
and combed our hair in whatever way we knew
and looked in whatever direction we could
because nothing was really going on
in our lives –
no girls to love, no dreams to fulfill,
no fight to fight

around eight at night, the sky grew
pretty much dark
and we walked to that beer shop

Red Room Bar

and bought a bottle of beer
I think it was Tuborg

I remember my mother telling me a year ago,

'You are very intelligent, my boy.
Very intelligent.'

anyways, for the first time in my life,
I held a beer bottle in my hand and it was cold

'This can be lethal. Are you sure?'
Kail asked me

'I am not sure, but now it must be done,'
I said

Kail opened the bottle cap with his teeth
and took a gulp and gave the bottle to me

'It's so shit!' he said

I took a gulp and felt like defecating
then and there
the fluid was cold only at the surface
but inside, it was hot lava
flowing down my throat

'That's it. That's it. Return the bottle,'
I said to Kail

and we laughed and he lit a cigarette
and took a drag while looking right

Red Room Bar

I closed my eyes and felt
the jolt and the dizziness
but it was better and sweeter
than the constant migraine that I was having

we took turns and gulped down all of it
and sat at a nearby eatery that served
all kinds of animals
and we ordered one of them and ate it

now, more than a decade later,
Kail has gone to hell,
there are 54 empty beer bottles lying around
in my balcony

but I still remember that night when it began.

Red Room Bar

46. **Drinking can't make you interesting**

myself, Skril and two others
sitting in my red room bar

it was cabin number 26
again

and we were ordering beer after beer
and in the middle of all the mayhem,
Skril looked up at me and said,

'I haven't got any fucking money!'

and I laughed and said

'I know. Don't worry about it.
Just drink…'

and he was drinking again
that evening, he drank more than any of us

Mr. Officer was a fucking bore
even after drinking so much, he hadn't anything
interesting to say
I call him Mr. Officer
because he always dressed
like he was an officer of some kind
and he was never off duty

I looked off duty even when I was on duty!

Red Room Bar

that evening, we drank 14 beer bottles in all
and then we drove to an eatery
in Mr. Officer's Honda car
and I remember eating very little
because the beer had taken all the space
inside my skin

even my soul had gone from its place

the fourth one of us, a lanky guy
was sitting with his head in his hands
after he finished
two and a half beer bottles
and he said

'No more. No more. It's too much.
It's too fucking much.'

and he sat quietly for like two minutes
and suddenly
the devil took hold of him again
and he drained a full beer glass in one go
and put the beer glass down on the table
with a BAM

BAM BAM BAM we put our glasses down
as well
'Fucking hell! Pour me some more,'
he said
and then closed his eyes

and we were laughing all the time
and it was a good laugh after a really long time

Red Room Bar

and at one time, I was checking my wallet
for the money
and I was laughing again

Skril was preaching something about life
Mr. Officer was boring us with trivial details
like what happened at his workplace that day –
things like that

always the same things happen at a workplace

the lanky guy wasn't able to take it anymore
and he ran outside and returned after 10 minutes
and put his head down on the table

and the three of us continued drinking
and it was not before eleven at night
when Mr. Officer said to us

'You are my real friends,'

and he took out some cash from his pockets
and I took out the rest from my pockets
and paid the bar manager

and it was not before midnight
when Mr. Officer
dropped me back on the street from where
my home was a short walk

I got down the car,
opened my purse one more time,
looked at how empty it had become

Red Room Bar

my home was at the end of that street
and I looked neither left nor right

and tried walking straight.

Red Room Bar

47. **Nobody comes here on Mondays**

the year is 2014 or 2015
I own nothing
I am new here
I have just arrived
and I have heard the city has some great
beer pubs brewing their own shit

one night, after a long work day, I gather myself
and head to one such brew pub
it's quite near to my place
which is not much of a place

A 7-minutes' walk and you are there,
gazing at the red blue neon lights
and a long alley adorned
with trees on either side
a woman opens the gate and she is walking out
with her head on the shoulders of a man
a whiff of music escapes the closed hall
through the gate,
reaches my ears
it's not jazz or classical or blues
the singer isn't Cohen or Sinatra
and I hear no trumpets
it's some rock song from the 1980s

I keep walking and now the golden miniature
lights are visible,
bordering the entrance gate
the music is quite loud now

Red Room Bar

I am alone and I am happy to find this place

the year must be 2015
because 2016 was a dead year to me

I am looking around, a waiter walks to me

'Have you come alone?'

'Yes, I have,' I reply

in pubs and bars, I have always gone alone
I walk inside and occupy a corner
six-seater table
it's not crowded and the table is rectangular
and the seats are well cushioned
the music is so loud, it hurts my ears but I think
it will get better
after drinking a glass of freshly brewed beer

the city is bustling with cars and people
I look at my watch and register the time
as 8:30 night
except for the choice of music,
I find everything fine here

in ten minutes, the waiter brings a glassful
to my table
and with it, a bowl of fries and some green
leaves on top of fries
I look at the beer, its pitch black colour
and take a sip
what a burn! what a taste!

Red Room Bar

'It's good. Really good,' I tell the waiter

he nods and smiles, then walks away
with the empty tray in which he brought
all this to me

'It's so good,' I tell myself as I drink more
and munch the fries

the song has changed,
only it's just another rock song
from the 1980s
I close my eyes and finish drinking my beer

two couples open the entrance door
both women wearing something purple
both men in black suit
they stop just near the door, whisper something
to one other
and then walk out immediately

I am wearing pajamas and a t-shirt
with a round neck

it's Monday
nobody celebrates on Monday,
everybody is lying exhausted
in their reclining chairs, on sofas
in their lover's arms, annoyed at trivial things,
angered over nothing,
over their own incompetence

Red Room Bar

everybody is there and I am here,
ordering another glass of pitch black beer,
swimming silently with the song

'Anything else, sir?' the waiter
comes to me and asks

'No. I am fine. Why is nobody here?' I ask for
the sake of asking something

'Oh it's Monday, Mondays are like this.
Come on Friday, you won't find a place to sit.
Believe me. HA HA HA,' the waiter says

I smile and he goes away
I watch the six hefty cylinders standing
vertically, metal made,
connected to one another, gallons of beer
travelling through them
I get up from my seat and walk to them,
humming a song
the waiter walks to me and explains the process

'…and that's how the beer is made here…'

that's all I remember him saying

I am quite drunk and dizzy
I close my eyes and listen
and everything sounds sweet and divine
my heart has suddenly grown so big
it was never this big

Red Room Bar

I walk back to my seat, sit down,
put my head down
I finish my second glass
and then I pay the waiter

it's 11 at night
the roads are wet with rain
a handful of cars crawling around

all the men and women
are inside something or the other

I stuff my hands
into the pockets of my pajamas

and I start walking home.

Red Room Bar

48. **Too much**

back in those days, I was living in Pine City
and the year was 2015
and it was a beautiful city back then
unlike today when there's only pollution
and lot of people

I and Mr Pan, a complete drunkard
and a good friend back in those days,
went to this bar one Saturday
and the music was really good,
it was rock music but real rock music
and there was a poor DJ standing at one corner
and shuffling songs

'I could do that. I could be a DJ,'
I said to Mr Pan

'Yeah. Even I can be a DJ. He is just
changing songs,' Mr Pan said

and we laughed and ordered
a draught beer tower
it held 1.5 liters of beer
and we filled our mugs, they were huge
and we began drinking

we reached that bar at 12 noon
it was far from where we lived
and we had to catch a bus to go there
nobody went to that bar at 12 noon

Red Room Bar

and so it was quiet enough
and I really liked it
and the music was good
and the beer was fantastic

we ordered a platter of seafood
and it had all kinds of shit,
all roasted and dry but delicious

we ate and ordered something more
and kept drinking
and time flowed so smoothly,
it hadn't flown so smoothly in decades
there was no war in that place

soon the poor DJ left
and the music kept shuffling
on its own
and we kept drinking and eating

and soon it was 2 o'clock noon
and we ordered another pitcher of beer
and it took almost an hour to finish that one
because we were already so full of beer
and all kinds of food

but it didn't matter somehow because
the bar was just so great and the music
was something out of this world

we got up and walked
and just outside the main door
was a little space for smokers

Red Room Bar

we took out two cigarettes, lit them
and smoked and watched men and women
entering and coming out
of the bar and talking crap about this and that
and more men and women coming out
with glasses in their hands and drinking
from each other's glasses and dancing
and smoking

at 3 o'clock noon
everything in that place seemed lively

we sat on a stair and finished our cigarettes

and then we went inside and finished the
remaining beer
and paid the bill

and let me tell you this -
once you have paid the bill,
there's nothing much to do
by staying there

it's the end of celebration

so I caught another bus and travelled back
and Mr Pan went on his way
to his brother's house
that was no so far away from that bar

it was already 4:30 in the evening
and I was feeling so sleepy
when I got this phone call

and I was out of my head completely
and I said

'Which bar? Oh fine. Be there at 5…'

and I got down the bus midway
and took a cab to that bar
and I opened the cab door
and threw myself inside
and told my uber driver,

'Gillie's Bar'

'Fine. Aren't you already drunk?'

'I am totally fine. Just drive…' I replied
with my eyes closed, sweat on my forehead

the driver listened to me
and drove straight to the bar
it didn't take much time
I paid him and got down
and ran at once across the road
the traffic wasn't much at that time
and it was almost 5 evening
and I thought if I was late

I was the first one to reach there
the others arrived there half an hour later
the bar was just opening up,
they hadn't even turned on the loudspeakers
and once they did, all they played
was shit pop music

Red Room Bar

it killed half the mood at once

anyways, I occupied a stool
and the others too,
all eight of us including me
and they ordered lime and rum
and I ordered a pint of beer

'A pint? That's all?' asked one of them

'Yes. That's all. You have no idea
how much I have drunk,'
and I told them about the day's drinking

after finishing the beer, I wanted to shit
so I ran to the bathroom
but it was already occupied
I banged on the door and some bitch
shouted from within

'Fine!' I shouted and went back to my stool
and few minutes later, I ran back
to the bathroom
and shitted like it was the last shitting of my life
and then, I went back to my stool
and finished my beer and ordered another pint
and some snacks and I was feeling really better
by that time

and I thought,

'I have drunk a lot today!'

Red Room Bar

and the more I thought about it,
the more unbelievable it seemed

I hadn't been so much drunk in my life before

we finished drinking by 7 o'clock
by which time, it was getting dark
and men and women started coming
in large numbers and almost all the
tables were occupied

'Care to smoke some weed?' asked one of them

'Sure. It's been a while…' I replied

so we got on the motorcycles and drove to
a house of one of them
and we locked the door and inside,
it was a hell of a place
so untidy and totally messed up

we sat in a room
and one of them started rolling weed
and others were talking shit or talking on phones
or just sitting there drunk and lost
and soon we lit a joint and smoked
and we turned off the lights
and turned on some blue neons and in no time,
we were dancing and jumping
and shouting and smoking
and beating each other and throwing each other
on each other and we were laughing so hard
and hugging each other

Red Room Bar

and dancing and dancing
and everything inside me was beginning to hurt
and I felt like throwing up but I guess I didn't
throw up
and I stopped dancing

I sat in one corner and I was crying
for whatever reason
the others continued to dance and smoke

'Need to leave now. Been a long day,'
I told the only friend I had
among all of them

'Fine. I understand. Should I drop you?'

'Not really. I will take a walk,'

I shook his hands
and opened the main door
and closed it behind me

I walked downstairs
it was a really huge society
having tens of multistory residential buildings,
all identical
and facing the same direction
I walked out of the main entrance,
walked a few metres
checked my wallet
I couldn't walk anymore
I was just too tired and too sad and too happy
I took a cab and went home straight

Red Room Bar

and I reached home

and I locked myself inside
for two whole days.

Red Room Bar

49. **You have no idea**

lots of smoke and beer
and cigarette butts getting tossed away
lots of sitting and drinking
and waiting for the right time to leave
lots of writing in between
all that drinking
and after the drinking is over
because life is burning away so fast
and you know that clearly
when you are a little out of your head
and you are trying really hard since a long time
and you still have no idea
if you are ever going to make it.

Red Room Bar

50. **I drove straight home**

I was smoking and drinking my usual
when I heard a man calling my name

by that time I was a regular in that bar

everybody knew me and they knew
what I would drink and eat
sometimes, the waiter ordered for me
even before I ordered for myself

it had become like that and I was fine with that
it was a nice gesture on their part and I guess
because of that, I didn't really go
to any of the other bars
there weren't many bars there, maybe 4 or 5
and they all looked similar

so I was drinking and smoking my usual
when I heard a man call my name

I thought my ears were ringing
I knew of a man who had such a problem
his ears would start ringing for no reason
that's what he used to tell everybody
one day, he was taken to a doctor
but it turned out the doctor
had the same problem
his ears would ring too
so the man thought, if he can be a doctor
then why can't I be a doctor

Red Room Bar

and I don't know what happened of him

so I was drinking and smoking my usual
when I heard somebody call my name

MR RITER? MR RITER?

MR RITER? ARE YOU THERE?

WHERE ARE YOU, MR RITER?

I didn't say a word
I was just listening and smoking and drinking

it was a man's voice

soon the man entered my cabin
saw me drinking and smoking and laughed
I was laughing as well
I had told the world I had quit drinking
and there I was, drinking like a drunk

he sat in the bench opposite to mine
he was laughing without stopping
I was laughing too and I said

'What happened?'

'Nothing. Nothing.
I knew I would find you here,'
he said and we both burst into laughing

'Where else would I be?' I replied

Red Room Bar

'Right. Right.'

'Want a beer?' I asked

'Oh no. My kid is outside. I better go now.
You have a good time. Call me
if you need anything.'

'I will.'

he left and I was alone again
drinking and smoking
I saw the time - 8:30 night
it was a full moon night and I didn't care

I asked waiter to bring the bill
and before he came back with the bill,
I sneaked out
and walked few hundred metres to take a piss
because I really needed to take a piss

but it wasn't before 9 when I returned to the bar
and by that time, all the lights went off
so I walked to the backdoor
and it was slightly open
and I entered and inside, four or five men
were still there,
drinking and smoking
I walked inside and crossed that room
and went to the billing counter

'Where the hell were you gone?'
asked the bar manager

Red Room Bar

'Went to pee.'

'HA HA. Fine.'

'How much?'

'635 bucks!'

'635?'

'Yes, 635' he said and he showed me
the full bill
and what item had cost how much

I was looking at it with much attention
but in reality, I wasn't able to see shit

'Good. No problem,' I said
and I paid the manager

and I walked out of there through the backdoor
I got on my bike, started it

and I drove straight home.

Red Room Bar

THE BOOK ENDS HERE

AND NOW

**HEADING BACK
TO MY RED ROOM BAR**
...

Printed in Great Britain
by Amazon

63865324R00130